FAMOUS
ROBBERIES
THE WORLD'S MOST
SPECTACULAR HEISTS

SOLEDAD ROMERO MARIÑO
& JULIO ANTONIO BLASCO

LITTLE
GESTALTEN

IMPRINT

Famous Robberies
The World's Most Spectacular Heists

Illustrated by Julio Antonio Blasco
Written by Soledad Romero Mariño

Translation from Spanish by
Emily Plank
Edited by Marilyn Knowlton
Typesetting by Mike Goulding

Printed by Schleunungdruck GmbH,
Marktheidenfeld
Made in Germany

Published by Little Gestalten,
Berlin 2022
ISBN 978-3-96704-728-8

The Spanish original edition
Robos de Leyenda was
published by Zahorí Books
© Zahorí Books, 2020
© Texts: Soledad Romero Mariño
© Illustrations: Julio Antonio Blasco
© for the English edition:
Little Gestalten, an imprint of
Die Gestalten Verlag
GmbH & Co. KG, Berlin 2022

For more information, and
to order books, please visit
www.little.gestalten.com

Bibliographic information published
by the Deutsche Nationalbibliothek.
The Deutsche Nationalbibliothek
lists this publication in the Deutsche
Nationalbibliografie; detailed
bibliographic data are available
online at www.dnb.de

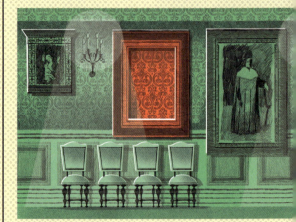

20 HOLD-UP OF A BOEING 727 BOUND FOR SEATTLE

A NONDESCRIPT GUY BOARDS THE PLANE AND PARACHUTES OUT WITH $200,000 WORTH OF BOOTY.

26 ROBBERY OF THE BANK OF NICE VIA THE SEWERS

A BANK IN NICE OPENS TO FIND ITSELF TOTALLY CLEANED OUT, EXCEPT FOR A BITTER NOTE FROM THE THIEVES: **"NO WEAPONS, NO VIOLENCE AND NO HATRED."**

44 A HACKER CARRIES OUT AN ATTACK ON CITIBANK

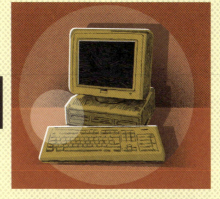

THE WORLD BANK AT THE MERCY OF A RUSSIAN TEEN.

56 BURGLARY AT FORTALEZA'S BANCO CENTRAL

A COLOSSAL FEAT OF ENGINEERING MAKES THIS BANK ROBBERY THE MOST SPECTACULAR IN BRAZIL'S HISTORY.

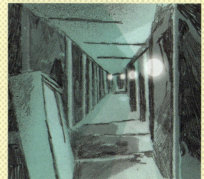

48 AUDACIOUS HEIST AT THE WORLD DIAMOND CENTRE

LA SCUOLA DI TORINO OUTWITS THE WORLD'S MOST SOPHISTICATED SECURITY SYSTEM AND STEALS A STASH OF PRECIOUS GEMS WORTH MORE THAN $100 MILLION.

LE
GRAND·PARISIEN

ILLUSTRATED **LITERARY** SUPPLEMENT

5 centimes · **5** centimes

Sixteenth Year · MONDAY, AUGUST 21, 1911 · No. 779

THE **MONA LISA** IS STOLEN FROM THE LOUVRE WITHOUT ANYONE REALIZING IT.

THE *MONA LISA* DISAPPEARS FROM THE LOUVRE

AN ITALIAN CARPENTER STEALS THE *MONA LISA* FROM THE MUSEUM IN BROAD DAYLIGHT

THE ROBBERY, ONE OF THE MOST FAMOUS EVER IN THE ART WORLD, PROMPTED THE ABSURD ARREST OF ARTIST PABLO PICASSO

WHEN:	WHERE:	WHO:	LOOT:	OUTCOME:
AUGUST 21, 1911	THE LOUVRE, PARIS, FRANCE	VINCENZO PERUGGIA	THE *MONA LISA* AKA *LA GIOCONDA*	PERUGGIA SPENT ONLY ONE YEAR AND 15 DAYS IN PRISON. HE WON THE HEARTS OF THE PEOPLE BY TREATING THE MASTERPIECE WITH RESPECT WHILE IT WAS IN HIS POSSESSION.

PLANNING THE ROBBERY

VINCENZO PERUGGIA

Peruggia was not your typical sophisticated, art-loving, white-collar thief. He was illiterate. He was born into a humble Italian family in the Lombardy town of Dumenza and had to leave his homeland to find work in France.

His early years in Paris were difficult, forcing him to commit several minor (and disastrous!) robberies. But as time passed, his ability to use his hands helped him land a job as a carpenter.

A FORMER LOUVRE EMPLOYEE

In 1910, the Louvre hired a team of four carpenters to produce glass showcases to protect the most coveted works of art.

Vincenzo Peruggia was one of those hired to do the job, and he and his coworkers added glass panels to the *Mona Lisa*, as well as to other works of art.

THE MUSEUM'S LACK OF SECURITY

Peruggia quickly noticed how lax the Louvre's security was, and despite being no genius, he felt he would easily be able to steal one of the works without attracting attention. It was just a question of taking advantage of the privilege he had been given to work there and, of course, having a bit of luck.

LITTLE SURVEILLANCE ON MONDAYS

On Mondays, the museum was always closed to the public for cleaning and maintenance. The lack of visitors made it an ideal time to photograph the works.

Monday was also the day in the week when the Louvre had the lowest level of security, with only 10 guards watching over the museum's works. For this reason, Peruggia decided to do his "deed" on a Monday.

A HUMBLE CARPENTER MANAGED TO EXPLOIT THE FLAWS IN THE MUSEUM'S SECURITY SYSTEM

VINCENZO PERUGGIA, PERPETRATOR OF THE FAMOUS MONA LISA ROBBERY IN 1911.

THE EMPTY SPACE WHERE THE *MONA LISA* SHOULD HAVE BEEN HANGING IN THE SALON CARRÉ (THE SQUARE SALON), ONE OF THE GALLERIES AT THE LOUVRE.

AN ITALIAN TREASURE

Of all the works, Peruggia chose the *Mona Lisa* because it was painted by an Italian artist and was a modest size (21 × 30 in). He had also heard an art expert say that it was one of the museum's greatest treasures. At the time, it was only the experts who considered it a masterpiece.

AT THE TIME, IT WAS ONLY THE EXPERTS WHO CONSIDERED IT A MASTERPIECE

A JEWEL

Florentine artist Leonardo da Vinci was commissioned by Francesco del Giocondo to paint the *Mona Lisa.* Giocondo wanted the great artist to create a portrait painting of his beautiful wife, Lisa Gherardini.

It took Leonardo four years to complete the extraordinary *Mona Lisa,* but for some reason, da Vinci did not deliver the painting as soon as he finished it.

The Italian genius painted the portrait in oil on wood. While the technique he used was innovative, what stood out most about the painting was its air of mystery.

The enigmatic smile and gaze of the female subject were somewhat disturbing, and the smoky landscape in the background was equally steeped in mystery. No one knew for sure where the exact location was.

The *Mona Lisa* was purchased by the French court in the early 1500s. Napoleon Bonaparte even had da Vinci's masterpiece installed in his wife's private quarters for a time.

PORTRAIT OF LISA GHERARDINI, THE WIFE OF FRANCESCO DEL GIOCONDO, BETTER KNOWN AS THE *MONA LISA* ("SIGNORA LISA," IN ITALIAN) OR *LA GIOCONDA.*

THE HEIST, STEP BY STEP

PERUGGIA STOLE THE PAINTING WITHOUT ANY ACCOMPLICES AND WITHOUT RAISING ANY SUSPICIONS

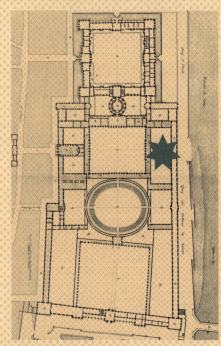

FLOOR PLAN OF THE LOUVRE WITH THE LOCATION OF LEONARDO'S PAINTING MARKED.

1. ENTERING THE MUSEUM

Although he had finished working at the Louvre several months earlier, Peruggia entered the museum bright and early on Monday, August 21, acting totally natural and dressed in a white worker's uniform.

He was a familiar face to the guards from the days when he had been adding glass panels to the works of art, so he did not raise any suspicions.

2. STEALING THE PAINTING

Peruggia made his way through several galleries before arriving at the Salon Carré. There on the wall was the *Mona Lisa*, vulnerable and without any surveillance. The carpenter had no trouble taking the painting down, since he was familiar with the hanging system. He took it to Visconti's spiral staircase, where he dismantled the frame and removed the glass panel. Then he placed a cloth over the painting for protection and calmly headed out.

3. LEAVING THE LOUVRE

Without attracting any attention, Peruggia made his way home with one of Leonardo da Vinci's masterpieces under his arm.

It was 8 a.m., and a humble, illiterate carpenter had just managed to commit the greatest art theft in history at the time.

4. CONFUSION AT THE MUSEUM

No one noticed that the painting was gone until the following day. It was Louis Béroud, a French artist, who was working on his own version of the *Mona Lisa*, who reported that the painting was missing.

At first, the Louvre's security staff did not believe that the painting could possibly have been stolen. Confusion reigned, but eventually they realized that Leonardo da Vinci's work had indeed vanished from Paris's most famous museum.

POLICE INVESTIGATION

THE MOST FAMOUS ART ROBBERY IN HISTORY

The museum reported the robbery at 11 a.m.

The incident soon made the front pages of every newspaper, and the police cordoned off the building in a desperate search for the painting. But it had already been several hours since the portrait's disappearance, and nobody knew exactly what had happened.

THERE WAS A GREAT SENSE OF DISQUIET IN THE ART WORLD

UNDER SCRUTINY

Peruggia was named as one of the prime suspects. He had worked for the museum and had a police record for some minor robberies committed during his early years in the French capital. He also had left the imprint of his left thumb on the frame.

Yet luck was on his side on this occasion because at the start of the 20th century, police took fingerprints from a person's right hand only, so the imprint of Peruggia's left thumb was of no help to them at all.

The investigation went around in circles following useless leads. Even the poet Guillaume Apollinaire and his colleague artist Pablo Picasso found themselves to be suspects of the robbery.

AFTER BEING STASHED AWAY FOR TWO YEARS, THE *MONA LISA* BECOMES THE WORLD'S MOST FAMOUS PAINTING

Many art lovers went to the Louvre just to gawk at the empty space where the painting had once been. The museum even boasted a record number of visitors.

The theft also prompted a number of forgeries of the famous portrait, which were intended to be sold to multi-millionaires.

In actual fact, however, the *Mona Lisa* spent two years stashed away in a humble Paris apartment. Vincenzo Peruggia, who was no doubt scared and unsure of what to do with the great work of art, kept it closely guarded under his bed—and continued leading his simple and unpretentious life as if nothing had happened.

PABLO PICASSO WAS ONE OF THE SUSPECTS, AS WAS THE POET APOLLINAIRE.

A PARIS POLICE PHOTOGRAPH OF VINCENZO PERUGGIA, PERPETRATOR OF THE THEFT OF THE *MONA LISA*.

THE DIRECTORS OF THE UFFIZI GALLERY IN FLORENCE TRICKED
PERUGGIA WHEN HE TRIED TO SELL THE MONA *LISA* TO THEM.

THE *MONA LISA* WAS FINALLY RETURNED TO THE LOUVRE, WHERE TODAY IT REMAINS PROTECTED BY BULLETPROOF GLASS. ONE OF THE MOST FAMOUS PAINTINGS IN THE WORLD, IT ATTRACTS MILLIONS OF VISITORS EVERY YEAR.

THE SALE AND RETURN OF THE WORK

Two years later, Peruggia, who finally wanted to enjoy the fruits of his labors, wrote a letter to the Uffizi Gallery in Florence, which was known to be interested in purchasing works by Renaissance artists.

PERUGGIA'S SENSE OF PATRIOTISM LANDED HIM IN PRISON

Under the pseudonym of Leonardo, Peruggia said that he wished to repatriate the *Mona Lisa* to Italy, where it had originally been painted.

The gallery did not take him seriously at first but responded nevertheless and invited him to Florence.

Peruggia put the *Mona Lisa* in his suitcase and traveled by train to meet the potential buyers, whom he arranged to receive in his modest hotel room. The visitors soon

realized that this was no joke; hidden in the carpenter's shabby little suitcase was indeed the real *Mona Lisa!*

THE PLOY

Promising Peruggia that the painting would be exhibited in Italy, the directors of the Uffizi Gallery took the *Mona Lisa* and betrayed the poor carpenter. They called the police, marking the end of the Italian thief's dream.

THE VERDICT

Peruggia spent one year and 15 days in an Italian prison. The *Mona Lisa* was returned to the Louvre's Salon Carré and became the world's most famous painting.

THE FILM

The German film drama *The Theft Of The Mona Lisa* (1931) is based on the life of Vincenzo Peruggia.

GLASGOW TIMES

Thursday, August 8, 1963   No. 18,556

IN THE QUIET CITY OF GLASGOW
THE GREAT TRAIN ROBBERY

A GROUP OF HOODED BANDITS ROB A GLASGOW TRAIN CARRYING 120 SACKS FULL OF BANKNOTES

THE BOOTY, WORTH £2.6 MILLION, MAKES THIS A LEGENDARY ROBBERY

SCOTLAND YARD SEEKS LEADS AFTER THE ROBBERY OF THE ROYAL MAIL TRAIN

PLANNING THE ROBBERY

A TIP-OFF ATTRACTS THE ATTENTION OF A SHREWD B-GRADE THIEF

BRUCE REYNOLDS OF LONDON (1931–2013)

Reynolds's early childhood was marked by very regular family conflict, and once he reached adolescence, he often got into fights.

Bruce spent his youth roaming the suburbs of the British capital, plotting and thieving, always trying to make it big until, inevitably, he ended up in jail.

IN DURHAM PRISON

While Reynolds was in jail, his cellmate told him a secret that would change his life forever. He disclosed to Reynolds the details of a special Royal Mail train that regularly transported sacks full of money from Glasgow's banks to the capital in the middle of the night.

That was the opportunity Reynolds had been waiting for, and from that moment on, he spent the rest of his jail time planning in detail the robbery of the loaded Royal Mail train.

WHEN:
AUGUST 8, 1963

WHERE:
THE LONDON-TO-GLASGOW MAIL TRAIN, NEAR BRIDEGO BRIDGE, UK

WHO:
A GANG OF 15 MEN, WITH BRUCE REYNOLDS AS THEIR LEADER

LOOT:
£2.6 MILLION STERLING (EQUIVALENT TO £43 MILLION STERLING IN TODAY'S MONEY, OR $50 MILLION)

OUTCOME:
SENTENCES OF AT LEAST 30 YEARS' IMPRISONMENT, ALTHOUGH SOME OF THOSE CONVICTED MANAGED TO ESCAPE JUSTICE AND BECAME FUGITIVES

THE ACTION BEGINS . . .

1 BRIDEGO BRIDGE

3:15 p.m., August 7, 1963
The mail train is intercepted on Bridego Bridge.
The robbers remove the sacks from the cars.

2 The gang drives two Land Rovers and one old military truck to a hideout.

3 LEATHERSLADE FARM

4:30 p.m.
The convoy arrives at the farm, where the robbers hide and divide up the loot.

THE HEIST, STEP BY STEP

BRUCE REYNOLDS—THE MASTERMIND.

A SINGLE BATTERY WAS ENOUGH TO STOP THE TRAIN

SOME OF THE GANG MEMBERS: **1.** WILLIAM BOAL, **2.** TOM WISBEY, **3.** ROGER CORDREY, **4.** JIM HUSSEY, **5.** ROY JAMES, **6.** BOB WELCH, **7.** JIMMY WHITE, **8.** RONNIE BIGGS, **9.** CHARLIE WILSON.

1. LONDON AND THE GANG

Bruce Reynolds completed his sentence and was released. He was finally able to carry out the plan he had been working on during his years in prison.

He traveled to London and gathered all the information on the Royal Mail train, then he recruited his gang members.

Reynolds carefully selected 14 good-for-nothing, criminal slackers to be his accomplices in the heist, based on each person's individual skills.

The gang was composed of these members: Douglas Gordon (alias Goody), Ronald Edwards (also known as Buster), Charlie Wilson, Ronnie Biggs, Roy James, Roger Cordrey, Tom Wisbey, Jim Hussey, Bob Welch, Brian Field, Leonard Field, Jimmy White, William Boal, and John Daly.

2. THE HIDEOUT

After years of preparation for the ambitious robbery, everything was set. There were just a few days to go, and the gang moved to what was to be the center of operations and their hideout: Leatherslade Farm, near Oakley, and the scene of the robbery.

3. THE NIGHT OF THE ROBBERY

The date chosen to commit the robbery was August 8, 1963.

That night, the mail train was to carry a staggering £2.6 million sterling—much more than the £300,000 it usually transported. It was a golden opportunity not to be missed.

4. BOARDING THE TRAIN

The train had 12 cars. It was guarded by 72 officers, and the money was kept in the second car. The train left Glasgow on time, but it never actually reached its destination.

The gang tampered with the signal battery at a spot 31 miles from London. The signal turned red, and the train stopped.

With their faces hidden under balaclavas, the robbers boarded the engine cab. The train driver resisted and was hit on the head (the only act of violence in the entire robbery).

ALL THE GANG HAD TO DO WAS TAMPER WITH A BATTERY TO TURN THE RAILWAY TRAFFIC SIGNAL RED: A SIMPLE BUT EFFECTIVE TRICK

BRIDEGO BRIDGE
IS THE SPOT WHERE THE
MAIL TRAIN WAS STOPPED
AND THE GREAT TRAIN
ROBBERY TOOK PLACE.

5. UNLOADING THE LOOT

Reynolds's gang unhitched the engine cab and the first two cars from the train, leaving the rest of the cars on the track.

They drove one mile to Bridego Bridge, where the rest of the gang was waiting on the highway.

Then they opened car number 2 and, forming a chain, loaded the sacks with the banknotes onto the truck within the space of only a few minutes.

Before leaving the crime scene, they warned the train officers not to report the incident for half an hour.

6. SAFE IN THE HIDEOUT

The gang now headed to their hideout. The plan was to wait for things to calm down before fleeing far from the reach of the authorities. Everything had gone as planned, and Bruce Reynolds had pulled off the robbery of the century.

WITHIN JUST A FEW MINUTES, THE GANG LOADED 118 OF THE 126 SACKS OF MONEY FROM THE TRAIN ONTO THEIR VEHICLE.

LEATHERSLADE FARM, WHERE THE GANG HID FOR THE FIRST FEW DAYS.

INVESTIGATION BY POLICE

AN ERROR LED THE POLICE TO THE GANG, WHO WERE SOON ALL ARRESTED

SCOTLAND YARD

The police arrived at the scene of the crime some 45 minutes later. The gang had completely ransacked the train without leaving a trace. All that remained in the car were eight pathetic sacks of money—along with the desperate, bewildered Royal Mail officers.

Around the world, newspapers were reporting the incident, and Scotland Yard assembled a special team to investigate.

Meanwhile, the robbers were lying low in hiding, eating pizza and playing Monopoly in their hideout at Leatherslade Farm.

THE BAND PLAYED MONOPOLY WITH REAL MONEY INSTEAD OF THE USUAL FAKE BILLS

IN THE TRASH, THE POLICE FOUND A MONOPOLY GAME THE GANG HAD BEEN PLAYING IN THEIR HIDEOUT.

KEY TO THE INVESTIGATION

The fact that the robbers had asked for 30 minutes to flee the scene before anyone called the police was Scotland Yard's first lead.

The detectives suspected the group had used the time to reach their safe house, and so they focused on combing the area in search of the thieves' hideout.

THE ROBBERS LEFT FINGERPRINTS ON A MONOPOLY GAME, A BOTTLE OF KETCHUP, AND SOME BEER CANS

SCOTLAND YARD LAUNCHED A WIDE-RANGING POLICE OPERATION TO INVESTIGATE THE CRIME. CHIEF SUPERINTENDENT JACK SLIPPER WAS IN CHARGE.

THE HIDEOUT

Several days went by, and the police continued to close in on the train robbers. Feeling uneasy about being discovered, the criminals divided up the money and fled their hideout.

The police finally located the hideout, thanks to a report they had received from one of the farm's neighbors. The robbers' fingerprints were everywhere. Also found was the irrefutable proof that tied them to the crime scene—the empty sacks of money.

THE OUTCOME

It wasn't difficult to find out whose fingerprints had been discovered at the farm hideout. All the train robbers already had police records for earlier crimes.

One by one, the gang members were arrested. At the trial, which lasted 51 days, they were sentenced to a minimum of 30 years in jail. Only one of the robbers, Ronnie Biggs, managed to escape. He went on to become a famous fugitive.

THE MINISERIES

The Great Train Robbery (2013) was a two-episode television miniseries based on this famous train robbery.

RONNIE BIGGS
A FAMOUS FUGITIVE

Despite being caught by the police, tried, and jailed, Biggs managed to escape from Wandsworth Prison soon after entering. In a great escape trail that went through France, Spain, and Australia, he made it as far as Brazil.

Ronnie lived in the South American country with his family for 31 years, becoming one of the UK's most famous fugitives. In 2001, he returned of his own free will to the country of his birth, where, after spending several years in prison, he was able to live as a free man until his death on December 13, 2013.

RONNIE BIGGS'S POLICE RECORD. FINGERPRINTS FROM HIS LEFT AND RIGHT HANDS.

Reno Evening Gazette

A Newspaper for the Home
Information and entertainment for every member of the family

R – No. 237   RENO, NEVADA, WEDNESDAY, NOVEMBER 24, 1971   PHONE FA 3-3161

$200,000 HAS DISAPPEARED

HIJACKING OF A BOEING 727
BOUND FOR SEATTLE

A NONDESCRIPT GUY BOARDS THE PLANE AND PARACHUTES OUT WITH $200,000 IN CASH

THE HIJACKER BECOMES A LEGEND. HIS "EXPLOITS" ARE CONSIDERED A TRIUMPH OF MAN OVER THE SYSTEM

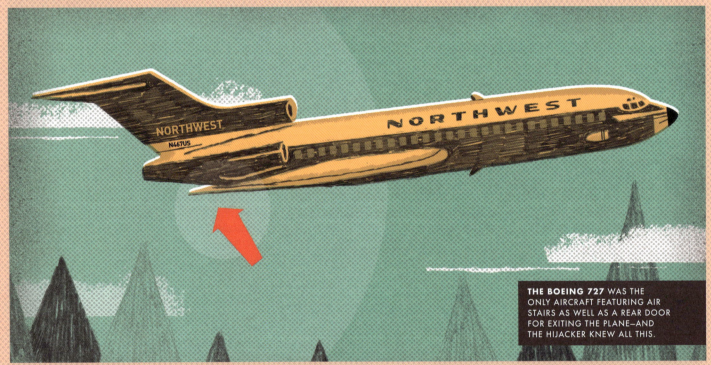

THE BOEING 727 WAS THE ONLY AIRCRAFT FEATURING AIR STAIRS AS WELL AS A REAR DOOR FOR EXITING THE PLANE—AND THE HIJACKER KNEW ALL THIS.

WHEN:	WHERE:	WHO:	LOOT:	OUTCOME:
NOVEMBER 24, 1971	A BOEING 727 PLANE BOUND FOR SEATTLE, US	DAN COOPER WAS THE NAME THAT HAD BEEN USED TO BUY THE PLANE TICKET	$200,000 (IN 20-DOLLAR BILLS)	NEVER CAUGHT

PLANNING THE ROBBERY

NOT A THING IS KNOWN ABOUT HOW THE ROBBERY WAS ARRANGED

The hijacker was never found or identified. To this day, any information on how the robbery was planned is pure speculation.

THE HEIST, STEP BY STEP

THE MOST FAMOUS ROBBERY IN HISTORY BEGINS WITH A PLANE TICKET TO SEATTLE

DAN COOPER, TICKET IN HAND, BEFORE BOARDING THE BOEING 727 BOUND FOR SEATTLE.

1. AT PORTLAND INTERNATIONAL AIRPORT

On November 24, 1971, on Thanksgiving eve, a nondescript man of average height, around 45 years old, dressed in a dark suit, white shirt, tie, and dress shoes, bought a plane ticket to travel from Portland, Oregon, to Seattle, Washington. He was a handsome man who went by the name Dan Cooper.

2. FLIGHT 305 TO SEATTLE

Dan Cooper duly boarded his flight and sat in the last row. His seat was 18C, and he was on the plane with 36 other passengers and six crew members.

3. THE NOTE

Once the plane had taken off, Cooper handed a note to flight attendant Florence Schaffner, a pretty young woman of 23. She thought the passenger had given her his number and kept the note without thinking anything of it. But Cooper leaned over and insisted, "Miss, you'd better look at that note. I have a bomb."

The flight attendant then read the note: "I have a bomb in my bag. I will use it if necessary." The ransom note went on to demand $200,000 in unmarked bills as well as four parachutes.

Following Cooper's orders, Florence Schaffner went to the cockpit to inform the pilots of what was happening.

The hijacker then hid his face behind dark sunglasses to protect his identity and waited for his demands to be met.

> "I HAVE A BOMB IN MY BAG. I WILL USE IT IF NECESSARY"

4. THE DEMANDS

The plane's captain followed the hijacker's instructions and contacted the control tower in Seattle. He informed air-traffic control of the hold-up and the attacker's demands.

The head of Northwest Orient Airlines and the FBI were briefed immediately.

THE ORDERS THE CREW RECEIVED WERE VERY CLEAR: COOPERATE WITH THE HIJACKER AND MAKE SURE THERE REALLY IS A BOMB

5. THE BOMB

Cooper showed the contents of his bag to the flight attendant and convinced everyone that his threat was real. He also provided precise details concerning how he wanted to get the money and the parachutes once the plane had landed at Seattle-Tacoma International Airport.

IF HIS DEMANDS WERE NOT MET EXACTLY, HE WOULD NOT HESITATE TO BLOW UP THE PLANE

6. THE LOOT

Cooper ordered the pilot to fly over Seattle until the $200,000 in unmarked bills and the parachutes had been obtained.

While those on the ground raced against time, all was rather calm on the plane. The passengers weren't aware of what was actually happening around them, and Dan Cooper was smoking cigarettes and enjoying a whisky with lemon soda, which he intended to pay for like a perfect gentleman.

7. SEA-TAC AIRPORT

At 5:24 p.m., the sum of $200,000 and the four parachutes demanded by the hijacker had been gathered. The four parachutes (civilian style with manually operated ripcords) were obtained from the local parachuting school, and the bills had been photographed to record their serial numbers.

COOPER ALLOWED THE PLANE TO LAND. IT TOUCHED DOWN AT 5:39 P.M. AND CAME TO A STOP ON A DARK, QUIET PIECE OF TARMAC, AWAY FROM THE SNIPERS

A Northwest employee was told to deliver the money and the parachutes to one of the plane's flight attendants. After thoroughly inspecting the delivery, Cooper freed the 36 passengers and one of the two flight attendants.

8. AT AN ALTITUDE OF 10,000 FEET

At 7:40 p.m., the Boeing 727 took off once more and left Seattle for Reno, Nevada. Cooper took over the controls for altitude, speed, and the rest of the plane's technical data. He also insisted that the plane's rear door be kept clear.

THE BOEING 727 WAS THE ONLY AIRCRAFT TYPE THAT HAD A REAR DOOR

The plane was flying at an altitude of around 10,000 feet in the middle of the night during a fierce storm. Cooper hid the 11 pounds of 20-dollar bills on his body under his clothes and ordered the last flight attendant still on board to lock the cockpit with the rest of the flight crew. The time had come. The daring hijacker was about to complete his mission.

9. THE BIG LEAP

That was when Cooper opened the rear door and jumped out.

BENEATH WERE MOUNTAINS, GLACIERS, AND FORESTS THAT COULD EASILY END HIS HEIST OR NOT … AND THAT WAS THE LAST ANYONE WOULD EVER KNOW OF HIM

THE SUITCASE COOPER SHOWED TO FLIGHT ATTENDANT SCHAFFNER CONTAINED SIX RED DYNAMITE CARTRIDGES, A BATTERY, AND SOME COPPER WIRE. EXPERTS LATER CONCLUDED THAT THE BOMB WAS A FAKE.

COOPER JUMPED OUT OF THE PLANE VIA THE REAR DOOR. BELOW HIM WERE THE HUGE MOUNTAINS AND FORESTS OF WASHINGTON STATE.

POLICE INVESTIGATION

Military planes accompanied Cooper's Boeing, but a fierce storm made the army pursuit difficult, and the army pilots were unable to see when he parachuted out.

When the plane landed in Reno, Nevada, after two and a half hours, it was surrounded by a large number of FBI and local police. The captain of the plane advised them that Dan Cooper had jumped out at around 8:13 p.m.

The police boarded the plane in search of clues, but all they found was a tie with a mother-of-pearl tie clip, two of the parachutes Cooper had demanded, as well as eight cigarette butts. There was no trace of the bag containing the bomb or the money or the other two parachutes.

ALL THAT WAS FOUND IN THE PLANE WERE TWO PARACHUTES AND THE BLACK TIE. NOT ONE OTHER CLUE OR TRACE

THE IDENTIKIT IMAGE CREATED BY POLICE BASED ON WITNESS ACCOUNTS.

IDENTITY AND IDENTIKIT IMAGE

The FBI investigated more than 1,000 suspects—in vain. Cooper's knowledge of aerodynamics and parachuting initially led them to believe that he was military, but they eventually discounted this theory on account of the recklessness of his jump.

THE SEARCH

Over the following six weeks, the police combed the area where they believed Cooper might have landed. Yet they never found anything.

The police also tried to track the 20-dollar bills that made up his ransom money, but they were equally unsuccessful.

THE FBI AND THE LOCAL POLICE SPENT MANY DAYS CONDUCTING AN INTENSIVE SEARCH OF THE AREA.

END OF THE INVESTIGATION

EVERY TELEVISION CHANNEL IN THE US AND THE REST OF THE WORLD WAS TALKING ABOUT THE HIJACKING.

"Norjak" was the code name assigned to the case by the FBI. The feds concluded that Cooper had died during his parachute jump.

But this theory was never confirmed, since no body was ever found. The hijacker had simply vanished into thin air.

Having considered multiple hypotheses, the FBI ended up throwing in the towel.

Meanwhile, Dan Cooper became an idol of the people. A single man had managed to outwit the system with extraordinary bravery, style, and ingenuity.

EVERY TELEVISION CHANNEL IN THE US AND THE REST OF THE WORLD WAS TALKING ABOUT THE HIJACKING.

Lake Merwin

Lewis River

Columbia River

The route of Northwest Orient Airlines flight 305.

The area where Cooper is thought to have landed.

The spot where a child found some of the ransom bills in February 1980.

8 KM

Vancouver Lake

WASHINGTON

VANCOUVER

Columbia River

Washougal

Willamette River

PORTLAND

OREGON

MAP OF THE AREA WHERE DAN COOPER LIKELY LANDED.

SECURITY MEASURES

One of the most important consequences of the hold-up was a detailed revision and modification of the security systems used on commercial flights and at airports all over the world.

THE USE OF METAL DETECTORS AT AIRPORTS BECAME A KEY COMPONENT OF FLIGHT SECURITY

HIJACKED PLANES

Despite the various new security measures that were introduced, three further Boeing 727 planes were hijacked during the year following the Seattle attack—all using methods similar to Cooper's.

The FDA then began requiring a special rear-door security lever on all Boeing 727s.

THE SECURITY LEVER PREVENTING A PLANE'S REAR DOOR FROM BEING OPENED DURING THE FLIGHT WAS NOW CALLED THE *COOPER VANE*

NINE YEARS LATER

The only trace Dan Cooper appears to have left at all was found nine years later. In 1980, a young boy out picnicking with his family found one of the money packets. It contained $5,800 in 20-dollar bills, part of the $200,000 ransom cash that was slowly decomposing.

22 years—No.10 436–0.40   **22** PAGES

TUESDAY, JULY 20, 1976

nice-matin

NEWS FROM SOUTHEAST FRANCE AND CORSICA

DIRECTORS. EDITORS. ADMINISTRATION
214 Boulevard du Mercantour
06290 Nice, Cedex 3, France

A BANK IN NICE OPENS TO FIND ITSELF TOTALLY CLEANED OUT, WITH A BITTER NOTE FROM THE THIEVES:

"NO WEAPONS, NO VIOLENCE, AND NO HATRED"

A FANTASTIC "HEIST"

ALBERT SPAGGIARI
ALIAS BERT

Albert Spaggiari was born and raised in the French Alps. He developed a certain kind of wiliness from a young age by committing petty crimes. In his first robbery, he is said to have snatched a diamond for his girlfriend. Apart from being a small-time crook, he was also a romantic.

When he got older, Albert traveled the world seeking excitement and adventure. He was a paratrooper in the Indochina War and was also a member of the illegal OAS (Organisation de l'armée secrète). His clandestine activities in the OAS resulted in Spaggiari serving several stints in prison.

MUG SHOT FROM HIS TIME AS A MEMBER OF THE ILLEGAL OAS (ORGANISATION DE L'ARMÉE SECRÈTE). SPAGGIARI ENDED UP IN PRISON FOR JOINING ITS RANKS.

WHEN:	WHERE:	WHO:	LOOT:	OUTCOME:
BETWEEN JULY 16 AND 20, 1976	SOCIÉTÉ GÉNÉRALE BANK IN NICE, FRANCE	ALBERT SPAGGIARI AND HIS GANG	A BOOTY THAT WOULD BE WORTH MORE THAN $11 MILLION IN MONEY AND JEWELS TODAY	DURING THE TRIAL, SPAGGIARI JUMPED OUT THE WINDOW AND ESCAPED ON A MOTORCYCLE

THE SOCIÉTÉ GÉNÉRALE BANK IN NICE. WITHIN ONLY A FEW HOURS OF LEARNING THE NEWS OF THE BREAK-IN, THE OWNERS OF THE SAFE-DEPOSIT BOXES SHOWED UP AT THE NICE BRANCH TO FIND OUT WHAT HAD HAPPENED TO THEIR VALUABLES.

PLANNING THE ROBBERY

A DESIRE FOR ADVENTURE INSPIRES A BORED EX-SOLDIER

A QUIET LIFE

In 1974, after completing yet another prison term, Albert Spaggiari led an honest life in the coastal city of Nice. He owned a photography studio and lived in a small mountain cottage with his wife. But such tranquility, such normalcy, was not for this adventurer, and it didn't last too long.

THE IDEA

During a dinner with friends, one of them, who happened to be an employee at Nice's Société Générale bank, innocently commented that a sewage pipe ran directly beneath the bank's vault.

ONLY LATER DID SPAGGIARI'S NAIVE FRIEND DISCOVER THE DIRE CONSEQUENCES OF HIS COMMENT

Spaggiari's imagination soon ran wild, and he began plotting the robbery of the bank in Nice. His idea was to drill a hole in the vault's floor from that very sewage pipe. Nobody would expect an attack like that!

THE ROUTE OF THE UNDERGROUND PASSAGE RAN FROM NICE'S CENTRAL PLACE MASSENA TO THE SOCIÉTÉ GÉNÉRALE BANK BUILDING, PASSING BENEATH TWO OF THE CITY'S STREETS.

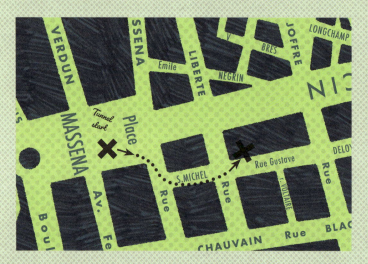

FROM NICE'S SEWER NETWORK, THE GANG BUILT A 43-FOOT-LONG TUNNEL, EXCAVATED ENTIRELY BY HAND IN AROUND TWO MONTHS.

THE HEIST, STEP BY STEP
A BANK ROBBED VIA THE SEWERS

1. SECURITY SYSTEMS

The first thing Spaggiari did was make sure that the vault's security systems wouldn't be capable of detecting any kind of drilling noises.

To do so, he rented a safe-deposit box at the bank. Inside it, he placed an alarm clock that was set to go off during the middle of the night.

The clock's vibration and alarm did not trigger any alarms in the building. Obviously, the vault, which was considered impenetrable, did not have a security system. Spaggiari's plan could work. He had the all-clear.

IT WAS EASY TO FIND A GANG OF 20 PROFESSIONAL CRIMINALS AND DEVISE A MASTER PLAN

2. THE GANG

Spaggiari next recruited his gang members. For this he contacted the Marseille mafia and some members of the OAS, the illegal group he had belonged to before going to prison.

3. TUNNELING IN THE SEWERS

Spaggiari and his criminal gang spent two months excavating a 43-foot-long tunnel through the sewers. It was a tough and rather smelly task. The thieves lugged heavy tools around the sewers and worked with military discipline as they carried out Spaggiari's perfect master plan.

4. ARRIVING AT THE VAULT

The men finally got into the vault on Saturday, July 16.

It was the weekend and the bank was closed to the public, so instead of having to blow up the vault at a specific time, Spaggiari and his gang were able to do so at their leisure.

While they inspected the contents of the safe-deposit boxes and chose what to take, they feasted on exquisite French wines, cheeses, and pâtés. They enjoyed a delicious weekend hold-up.

THERE IS NO DOUBT THAT SPAGGIARI'S MODUS OPERANDI AND CAUSTIC HUMOR MADE THIS ROBBERY A MASTERPIECE

5. THE LOOT

Spaggiari ordered his gang not to touch the safe-deposit boxes containing little money or people's personal savings. His crimes were not aimed at simple, hardworking folks. Instead, he affixed several compromising photographs of powerful figures to the vault's walls for all the world to see.

6. THE ESCAPE

On Monday morning, just before the bank opened its doors to the public, Spaggiari and his gang exited the vault and left a cryptic message scrawled on the wall, "No weapons, no violence, and no hatred."

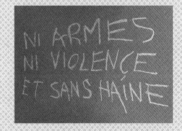

THE ROBBERS VOTED ON WHICH PHRASE THEY WOULD LEAVE SCRAWLED ON THE VAULT'S WALLS

The robbers carefully sealed the stolen cash in bags and transported it out via rafts that sailed on the waters of the sewage canal. This way, they didn't leave a single trace or clue for the police.

SPAGGIARI'S CALMNESS AND MOCKING SPIRIT MEANT HE WAS ABLE TO ENJOY HIS TIME IN THE BANK'S VAULT AND RELAX DRINKING FRENCH WINE.

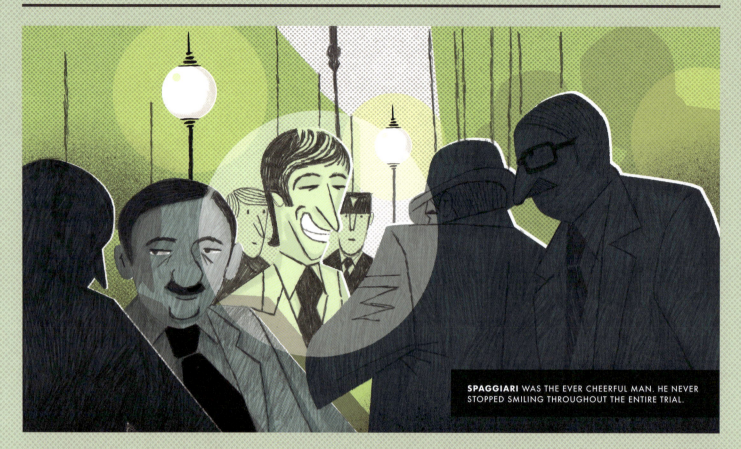

SPAGGIARI WAS THE EVER CHEERFUL MAN. HE NEVER STOPPED SMILING THROUGHOUT THE ENTIRE TRIAL.

POLICE INVESTIGATION & TRIAL

SPAGGIARI WAS A PECULIAR CHARACTER, CAPABLE OF TURNING A ROBBERY INTO A GREAT ADVENTURE

AN ACCOMPLICE WAS WAITING FOR HIM ON A MOTORCYCLE AT THE END OF THE STREET

There are various versions as to what led the police to Spaggiari, but whatever it was, there is no doubt the ex-soldier never got the jitters at the time of his arrest.

Throughout the trial, he laughed at the judges and told absurd stories based on his own fantasies. He beat around the bush and enjoyed the spectacle until, one day, in the middle of the trial, he suddenly jumped out the window, landed on top of a car, and escaped aboard a motorcycle.

THE FILM

The Sewers of Paradise (1971), directed by José Giovanni, is a French film recounting the fascinating adventure of Albert Spaggiari.

THE FUGITIVE

Spaggiari spent the rest of his days as a fugitive, and he greatly enjoyed his clandestine life. He granted secret interviews, wrote a book (*The Sewers of Gold*), and rubbed shoulders with other famous fugitives.

In one interview, he confessed that he had never wanted the bank's money and that his real motivation had been the challenge of the robbery itself and the idea of mocking the system.

HE SPENT THE TRIAL WALKING AROUND THE ROOM, GIVING RIDICULOUS REPLIES TO EVERY QUESTION AND CREATING FANTASIES THAT MIXED TRUTH WITH LIES

His escape happened at lightning speed. Nobody saw Albert Spaggiari or his wife ever again—nor any part of the substantial booty he escaped with, the amount of which broke all records.

THE MODERN ROBIN HOOD SENT 5,000 FRANCS TO THE UNFORTUNATE OWNER OF THE CAR HE FELL THROUGH AFTER JUMPING OUT THE WINDOW.

EL PAÍS

MADRID EDITION   INDEPENDENT DAILY NEWSPAPER   JULY 28, 1989

A GUARD FROM A SECURITY COMPANY ROBS AN ARMORED TRUCK CARRYING 320 MILLION PESETAS

A DREAM ESCAPE

OVERNIGHT, AN ANONYMOUS WORKER BECOMES EL DIONI, SPAIN'S MOST FAMOUS FUGITIVE MILLIONAIRE

WHEN:
JULY 28, 1989

WHERE:
MADRID, SPAIN

WHO:
DIONISIO RODRÍGUEZ MARTÍN, NICKNAMED EL DIONI

LOOT:
320 MILLION PESETAS ($2.23 MILLION)

OUTCOME:
ACCUSED OF MISAPPROPRIATION, HE WAS SENTENCED TO THREE YEARS AND FOUR MONTHS IN JAIL

THE ARMORED TRUCK BELONGING TO THE SPANISH COMPANY CANDI S.A., WHERE EL DIONI WORKED AS A SECURITY GUARD ON JULY 28, 1989.

PLANNING THE ROBBERY

DIONISIO RODRÍGUEZ MARTÍN
ALIAS EL DIONI

EL DIONI WAS AN ENTHUSIASTIC YOUNG MAN. HE WANTED TO DO GOOD, SERVE SOCIETY, AND DEFEND THE LAW

Dionisio Martín started his career working as a security guard, but his energy and dedication quickly helped him get promoted to the position of bodyguard.

THE BODYGUARD

El Dioni was thought to be among of the country's best bodyguards. But one fateful day, a client whom he was protecting died in a strange accident, ruining El Dioni's reputation.

His boss at the security company Candi S. A. promptly demoted him to the position of driver.

AT THE WHEEL OF ARMORED TRUCKS

Martín's new role would be to drive the company's armored trucks.

El Dioni had gone from earning 250,000 pesetas and wearing a stylish bodyguard suit to earning just 70,000 pesetas and wearing a second-rate blue driver's uniform.

THE VALLE DEL NARCEA CAFETERIA

It was a huge blow for El Dioni. He tried everything possible to get his previous job back, but he was unsuccessful.

El Dioni became angry, and one day at the Valle del Narcea café, he told his friends that he was going to rob an armored truck. So goes the legend . . . And that same evening, El Dioni decided to take the law into his own hands.

EL DIONI BECAME ANGRY, AND ONE DAY AT THE VALLE DEL NARCEA CAFÉ, HE TOLD HIS FRIENDS THAT HE WAS GOING TO ROB AN ARMORED TRUCK

EL DIONI WAS USED TO FREQUENTING BARS AND HAVING A FEW DRINKS AFTER WORK.

THE HEIST, STEP BY STEP

1. THE ROUTE

That night, El Dioni worked, as always, alongside his two Candi colleagues. They drove around the city collecting their clients' money. The truck didn't carry an exceptional amount of cash—in fact, the day before, it was carrying twice as much—which made people suspect that El Dioni acted on impulse.

2. THE RAID

On their last stop, while his accomplices were collecting the profits from the Pastelería Mallorca patisserie, El Dioni put his foot on the gas and took off.

A SIMPLE AND EFFECTIVE HEIST. HE LEFT HIS COLLEAGUES AND DROVE OFF WITH A TRUCK FULL OF MONEY

EL DIONI TOOK THE TRUCK FROM OUTSIDE THE PASTELERÍA MALLORCA PATISSERIE, LOCATED ON CALLE DE ALBERTO ALCOCER IN CENTRAL MADRID, SOMETIME BETWEEN 7:15 P.M. AND 7:45 P.M. HE THEN DROVE 760 YARDS DOWN THE ROAD TO CALLE MAESTRO LASSALLE, WHERE HE HAD PARKED HIS OWN CAR, A BLUE AUDI 80 WITH THE LICENSE PLATE M-7682-DG.

3. ESCAPE IN MADRID

The ex-bodyguard drove the truck from the city center to his car. He was frantically being called on the company radio. His heart was racing fast, but he ignored the calls and simply stuck to his plan.

WHEN HE ARRIVED AT HIS CAR, HE LOADED THE BAGS FILLED WITH 320 MILLION PESETAS INTO THE TRUNK AND LEFT THE TRUCK IN THE MIDDLE OF THE STREET

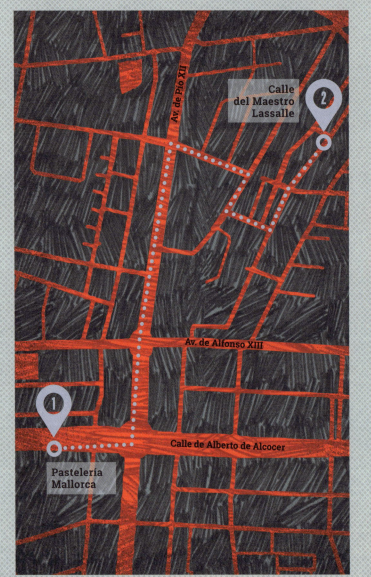

Calle del Maestro Lassalle

Av. de Pío XII

Av. de Alfonso XIII

Calle de Alberto de Alcocer

Pastelería Mallorca

4. THE ACCOMPLICES

His friends were waiting for him at the truck yard. They were Jesús Arrondo (alias Cocoliso, a spy with the terrorist organization ETA), Miguel Ángel Dueñas (his child's godfather), and Jorge Medina (alias Patagón and one of Spain's military intelligence collaborators).

THEY DIVIDED UP THE MILLIONS QUICKLY, EACH TAKING HIS SHARE

5. THE HIDEOUT

As the news of the armored truck robbery spread like wildfire across the media, El Dioni hid in the home of friends, a married couple. Overnight, the robber went from being an anonymous security guard to Spain's most wanted fugitive.

THE COMPANY WAS FORCED TO CLOSE, WHILE HE CELEBRATED HIS TRIUMPH WITH CHAMPAGNE AND CAVIAR IN HIDING

6. A NEW LIFE IN BRAZIL

Once things calmed down, El Dioni fled to Brazil, where he put on a wig and started a new life in style. He lived lavishly at the Barra Palace Hotel-residência in Rio de Janeiro, traveled by private jet, and was chauffeured around the city in a limousine.

EL DIONI WAS A HAPPY, CHATTY GUY, LIVING EVERY WORKING MAN'S DREAM

THE VIEW FROM HIS ROOM AT THE BARRA PALACE HOTEL-RESIDÊNCIA IN RIO DE JANEIRO.

POLICE INVESTIGATION

WHAT THE PRESS SAID

However, El Dioni's life of luxury attracted attention, and the Brazilian police soon started investigating.

In his hotel room, they found a stash of contraband goods, a couple of handguns, and various press clippings about his escape in the armored truck.

EL DIONI HAS BEEN DISCOVERED!

THE NEWSPAPER CLIPPINGS EL DIONI KEPT IN HIS HOTEL ROOM WERE FOUND BY THE POLICE.

SE BUSCA

POLICIA NACIONAL   📞 TLFN. 091

DIONISIO RODRIGUEZ MARTIN

SPANISH POLICE STUCK UP WANTED POSTERS OF EL DIONI'S FACE TO TRY TO FIND HIM.

PRISON IN BRAZIL

The Brazilian police tried to find the stolen money, but El Dioni claimed that it was still in Spain. The lie is probably what saved his life.

ON SEPTEMBER 19, 1989, THE WORLD'S MOST FAMOUS FUGITIVE AT THE TIME ENTERED A BRAZILIAN JAIL

Ten months later, the fugitive robber was extradited to Spain.

BACK HOME

One year after his great robbery, El Dioni was on his way back to Spain. The captain of the plane told the passengers that they were taking El Dioni "home," and everyone applauded.

SPAIN WELCOMED HIM LIKE A HERO

As El Dioni entered jail, the inmates applauded. The robber had become a kind of antihero, a cult figure for the poor and the working class.

OUTCOME

El Dioni was fortunate at his trial. While his story had many flaws, he had taken the armored truck and the money without hurting anyone.

THE JUDGE RULED MISAPPROPRIATION, SENTENCING HIM TO THREE YEARS AND FOUR MONTHS IN PRISON

EL DIONI, GUARDED BY TWO AGENTS ON HIS RETURN TO SPAIN.

140 MILLION PESETAS GONE

El Dioni claimed he had robbed the security truck on his own, that he was the only one responsible, and that he knew nothing about his friends or the 140 million missing pesetas.

The police were able to locate only Miguel Ángel Dueñas's share of the stolen money, which he kept in a secret compartment behind a closet in his home. Nobody ever found out where the rest of the money was.

As for the ex-bodyguard's other two accomplices, Jesús Arrondo had died in a mysterious accident, and Jorge Medina had vanished forever with his handsome share of the money.

El Dioni has, in fact, always maintained that Medina was the brightest of all those involved in the robbery.

LEAVING JAIL

In May 1995, El Dioni left jail on parole after completing three-quarters of his prison term. He claimed not to have a single céntimo, and didn't have to pay back the 140 million pesetas that had gone missing.

On the street, El Dioni had become an urban legend. People would ask for his autograph, and when asked, he would say with a big grin that he was not sorry about what he had done.

"HE WOULD COMMIT THE ROBBERY AGAIN, BECAUSE … THE ONES WHO SHOULD SET AN EXAMPLE OF HONESTY AND INTEGRITY ARE THE ONES WHO ENCOURAGE ROBBERIES"

The Boston Globe

SUNDAY, MARCH 18, 1990

HISTORIC ART ROBBERY
AT THE ISABELLA STEWART GARDNER MUSEUM

DISGUISED AS POLICE OFFICERS, TWO THIEVES STEAL 13 WORKS OF ART WORTH $500 MILLION FROM THE ISABELLA STEWART GARDNER MUSEUM

REGARDED AS THE GREATEST ART ROBBERY IN US HISTORY, THE FBI HAS YET TO SOLVE THE CASE

BOSTON'S ISABELLA STEWART GARDNER MUSEUM. THE EMPTY FRAME PROTECTED A FAMOUS STOLEN WORK OF ART BY DUTCH PAINTER REMBRANDT.

WHEN:	WHERE:	WHO:	LOOT:	OUTCOME:
MARCH 18, 1990	THE ISABELLA STEWART GARDNER MUSEUM IN BOSTON, MA, US	TWO MYSTERIOUS AND CLEVER THIEVES	13 WORKS OF ART WORTH $500 MILLION	THERE WAS NO TRIAL. THE FBI NEVER MANAGED TO IDENTIFY THE THIEVES

THE ISABELLA STEWART GARDNER MUSEUM

PORTRAIT OF ISABELLA STEWART GARDNER, AMERICAN PATRON AND ART COLLECTOR.

ITS PAINTINGS, SCULPTURES, TAPESTRIES, FURNITURE, AND OTHER PRECIOUS DECORATIVE ITEMS WERE A SERIOUS TEMPTATION FOR THE THIEVES

Isabella Stewart Gardner was an extraordinary woman and ahead of her time in many respects. She was fortunate to have had a good education and be able to travel the world.

On a visit to Italy, Isabella befriended some great artists who sparked her passion for art. When she returned to the US, still inspired by her unforgettable Italian experience, Isabella converted her Boston mansion into a thoroughly charming Renaissance-style museum.

The Isabella Stewart Gardner Museum was soon admired for its warm, homey atmosphere and the exquisite collection of paintings, textiles, and furniture that its creator had acquired from European, Asian, and American artists.

PLANNING THE ROBBERY

AN INGENIOUS OPERATION THAT LEFT FEW CLUES FOR THE POLICE

The few traces left behind by the thieves were not clear enough for investigators to obtain details on how the robbery had been planned. In any case, the police declared that it had been plotted several months in advance. The burglars knew everything about the museum and its state-of-the-art security systems.

BOSTON'S ISABELLA STEWART GARDNER MUSEUM. ITS DESIGN WAS INSPIRED BY RENAISSANCE PALACES.

THE HEIST, STEP BY STEP

ONE RAINY NIGHT IN MARCH, TWO THIEVES DISGUISED AS POLICE OFFICERS SHOW UP AT THE MUSEUM

CHRIST IN THE STORM ON THE SEA OF GALILEE, BY REMBRANDT.

1. A FAKE INCIDENT

Soon after midnight on March 18, 1990, two police officers appeared at the front door of the Isabella Stewart Gardner Museum. They explained that they had come to investigate a "suspicious noise" and that they needed to enter the museum to make sure everything was all right.

The building's young and inexperienced security guard, Richard "Rick" Abath, did not doubt the fake officers' story for a second.

Who would ever suspect uniformed police officers? So, breaching all security protocols, the guard unwittingly let the two criminals in.

2. "GENTLEMEN, THIS IS A HOLD-UP"

Once inside the building, the supposed police officers pulled out their guns and revealed their true intentions to the museum's two security guards.

WEARING POLICE UNIFORMS AND HIDDEN BEHIND BUSHY FALSE MUSTACHES, THE ROBBERS MANAGED TO DECEIVE THE MUSEUM'S SECURITY STAFF

3. TIED UP IN THE CELLAR

The robbers took the security guards to the museum's cellar rooms, where they gagged them with adhesive tape and handcuffed them to the heating pipes. One obstacle overcome.

4. THE ALL-CLEAR

Undisturbed, the two bandits next went about disabling all of the museum's state-of-the-art security systems. They covered the cameras and freely moved through the halls of the museum for an astonishing 81 minutes, choosing the works and objects they wanted to take.

THE CONCERT, BY JOHANNES VERMEER.

CHEZ TORTONI, BY ÉDOUARD MANET.

A LADY AND GENTLEMAN IN BLACK, BY REMBRANDT.

5. DUTCH ROOM

The Dutch Room, on the second floor, was target number one. The robbers took several works off the walls and removed their frames. They indiscriminately cut some of the canvases so that the art could be taken out of their heavy protective casings.

Loaded up with the works and leaving the empty frames behind, the thieves made their way around the museum.

The robbers chose six pieces from the Dutch Room:

3 works by Rembrandt:
The famous *Christ in the Storm on the Sea of Galilee* (the only seascape painted by the artist), *A Lady and Gentleman in Black* and a *Self-portrait* barely larger than a postage stamp.

1 painting by Vermeer:
The Concert (Dutch: *Het concert*) one of the artist's 36 (and few) recognized works.

1 painting by Flinck:
Landscape with Obelisk, a work that had been attributed to Rembrandt until the 1970s.

1 ritual bronze Chinese vase from the Gu Dynasty:
A piece from the 12th century BC, and somewhat incongruous with the rest of the booty.

5 drawings by Degas: Three depicted riders on horseback, and the other two were sketches for an art event program.

Bronze eagle-shaped finial of Napoleon's Imperial Guard: Yet another incongruous choice by the robbers.

7. BLUE ROOM

The Blue Room finally was the robbers' third and last stop. Located on the first floor, the works of great American and French artists, such as Sargent, Delacroix, Corot, and Courbet, were exhibited here. But strangely the thieves took only one single, small work:

1 oil painting by Manet: *Chez Tortoni*, a portrait of a man sitting in a Parisian café.

STRANGELY, THIS PAINTING'S FRAME WAS THE ONLY ONE THE ROBBERS DIDN'T LEAVE IN THE ROOM. THEY DARINGLY PLACED IT ON THE CHAIR IN THE SECURITY MANAGER'S OFFICE

LANDSCAPE WITH OBELISK, BY GOVERT FLINCK.

6. SHORT GALLERY

The next gallery to be tackled by the art thieves was the so-called Short Gallery, which was also located on the second floor of the museum building.

To get there, the robbers first had to pass through the galleries of the Italian artists.

Inexplicably, the fake police officers had to walk right past some extremely valuable Italian paintings, yet they failed to stop and remove any of them. Instead, they went straight to the Short Gallery, where they stole:

8. THE ESCAPE

Surprisingly, the criminals did not go up to the third floor, which housed one of the museum's real treasures: *The Rape of Europa*, by Venetian painter Titian.

The robbers left the galleries, took the videotapes and reports from the motion sensors, and deemed their mission complete.

They had taken what they wanted from the museum within 81 minutes. At around 2:45 a.m., the fake police officers exited the building separately and were never seen again.

IN THE EARLY HOURS OF MARCH 18, 1990, THE TWO ROBBERS CALMLY LEFT THE MUSEUM, EACH GOING HIS OWN WAY. THEY LOADED ALL THE STOLEN PIECES INTO TWO TRUCKS AND DISAPPEARED.

POLICE INVESTIGATION

AT DAYBREAK

The art theft at the Gardner Museum was not discovered until 8 a.m. the next day when the day-shift security guards found their colleagues gagged and handcuffed in the basement.

THE GUARDS HAD SPENT THE WORST NIGHT OF THEIR LIVES, AND THE MUSEUM HAD SUFFERED THE LARGEST ART ROBBERY IN US HISTORY

TRACES OF THE ROBBERS' MOVEMENTS

When the real police arrived at the museum, they were able to recover only recordings of the thieves' movements on a computer's hard drive, which the thieves hadn't thought to delete. There were no other clues.

THE CRIMINALS HAD DONE A CLEAN JOB, SECURING BOOTY WORTH MORE THAN $500 MILLION

PROFESSIONAL ROBBERS

The burglars' modus operandi and knowledge of the alarm systems left the police investigators in no doubt that they were dealing with professionals.

ON THE OTHER HAND, THE PECULIAR CHOICE OF WORKS AND THE UNDIGNIFIED MANNER IN WHICH THE PAINTINGS HAD BEEN REMOVED FROM THEIR FRAMES ALSO LED THE POLICE TO SUSPECT THAT THE THIEVES WERE NOT ART EXPERTS

SUSPECT 1 — YOUNG MAN — DISGUISED
SUSPECT 2 — YOUNG MAN — DISGUISED

A PUZZLE

If the thieves had little knowledge of art, perhaps the mafia was involved in this very peculiar robbery. Had it been an assignment? Had there been a list of works to steal or had they chosen them on the spot? Why didn't they take the museum's most important Italian paintings? Had it been a last-minute whim to steal the bronze Gu vase and the finial?

THE POLICE WERE PUZZLED BY MANY QUESTIONS, BUT THERE WERE NO ANSWERS

THE REWARD

The lack of evidence and the remote possibility of recovering any of the works of art prompted the museum to offer a big reward to anyone able to provide information.

THE ISABELLA STEWART GARDNER MUSEUM WOULD PAY $5 MILLION FOR ANY INFORMATION LEADING TO THE RECOVERY OF THE MISSING ART. IN 2017, THIS SUM WAS DOUBLED TO $10 MILLION, AND IT IS STILL BEING OFFERED TODAY

For some time, the museum left the empty frames of the stolen paintings hanging on the walls as symbols of its confidence that they would be returned. But the gesture didn't work.

POLICE FAILURE

Today, three decades later, the art robbers are yet to be found and tried.

THIS ROBBERY IS ONE OF THE GREATEST MYSTERIES IN THE WORLD OF CRIME, A ROBBERY OF INCALCULABLE ARTISTIC VALUE

The New York Times

VOL. CLXVI . . . No. 57,674   NEW YORK, THURSDAY, JUNE 30, 1994 $6.00

THE GLOBAL BANK AT THE MERCY OF A YOUNG RUSSIAN MATHEMATICIAN

A HACKER'S CYBERATTACK ON CITIBANK

PLANNING THE ROBBERY

A HACKER OUTWITS CITIBANK'S COMPUTER SECURITY SYSTEMS

VLADIMIR LEVIN

Having studied biochemistry and math at St. Petersburg University, Vladimir Levin was a science-minded man who was equally passionate about computers. Vladimir didn't hesitate to use his extraordinary talents in IT to attack the security systems of various banks around the world. He would spend hours at his computer working out strategies and combinations to outwit them.

VLADIMIR LEVIN DURING HIS UNIVERSITY YEARS IN ST. PETERSBURG.

WHEN:
JUNE 1994

WHERE:
FROM ST. PETERSBURG, RUSSIA, A HACKER ATTACKS CITIBANK, NEW YORK, US

WHO:
VLADIMIR LEVIN AND HIS GANG OF HACKERS

LOOT:
$10.7 MILLION

OUTCOME:
LEVIN WAS SENTENCED TO THREE YEARS IN PRISON AND HAD TO PAY CITIBANK $240,000

THE HEADQUARTERS OF **CITIBANK** IN NEW YORK CITY.

THE HEIST, STEP BY STEP

FROM HIS REMOTE OFFICE, ARMED ONLY WITH COMPUTER AND MODEM, THE YOUNG MAN ATTACKED THE AMERICAN BANKING GIANT

1. THE AO SATURN COMPANY

The pirate attack was started from the AO Saturn office in St. Petersburg, Russia, where a young Vladimir Levin worked at his computer connected to the Internet.

Working tirelessly and secretly, the innocuous young man dedicated himself to finding a way of taking down the security systems of banks.

2. LIST OF ACCOUNT NUMBERS AND PASSWORDS

Having put in many hours, much brainpower, and incredible patience, Levin finally cracked it. He had managed to get into Citibank's system from his office. He downloaded a list of checking accounts and passwords and, with minimal effort, transferred money from the bank's clients to his own account.

HE HAD THE GOOSE THAT LAID THE GOLDEN EGG

THE HEADQUARTERS OF THE COMPUTER COMPANY AO SATURN, IN ST. PETERSBURG, WHERE VLADIMIR LEVIN COMMITTED THE ATTACKS IN 1994.

THE YOUNG RUSSIAN HACKER, WHO WAS USING A STANDARD PERSONAL COMPUTER, WAS ABLE TO CRACK THE SECURITY SYSTEM OF ONE OF THE WORLD'S MOST SOPHISTICATED PAYMENT SYSTEMS.

3. A GANG OF HACKERS

Aware of the potential his success could bring, the young man formed an international gang of hackers.

Levin's strategy was to go for simultaneous attacks from all corners of the globe, moving the money from account to account until the trail was lost.

LEVIN ASSEMBLED A GANG OF HACKERS AND DEMANDED A RANSOM FROM THE WORLD BANK

4. SECRET ACCOUNTS WORLDWIDE

The network of hackers went on to transfer money to accounts in the US, Finland, Argentina, Germany, the Netherlands, and Israel. In a few weeks, they stole more than $10 million without leaving their seats.

AT THE TIME, BANKS AROUND THE WORLD WERE NOT AWARE THAT THEY WERE BEING ATTACKED

5. CRISIS AT THE BIG BANK

Levin and his accomplices demonstrated that the money deposited at these banks wasn't secure. The bank had suffered the greatest attack in its history and reported it to the police.

6. THE LOOT

Nobody could figure out how much money had been stolen or where it had ended up. The IT maze created by the hackers made it impossible to determine the scale of the robbery.

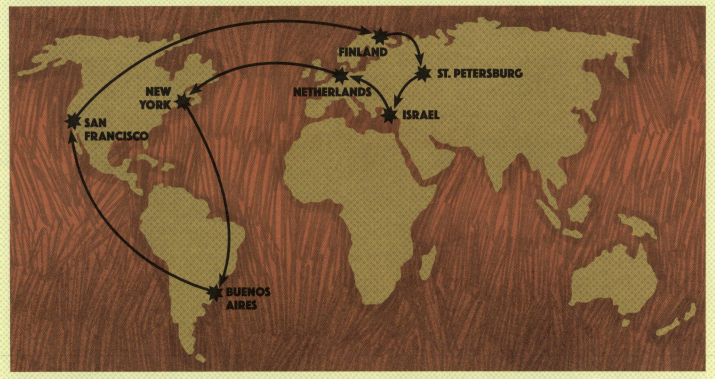

THE MONEY WAS TRANSFERRED TO MULTIPLE ACCOUNTS LOCATED IN THE US, FINLAND, ARGENTINA, THE NETHERLANDS, GERMANY, AND ISRAEL.

POLICE INVESTIGATION

INTERPOL ASSEMBLED A SPECIAL UNIT TO TRACK THE GANG'S MOVEMENTS AND APPREHEND ITS MEMBERS. THEY ANALYZED THE HACKERS' OPERATIONS IN MINUTE DETAIL

CAPTURE

It took Interpol quite a few months to capture the operation's mastermind.

Levin was eventually apprehended at one of the London airports as he was setting off to fly to a video game convention.

THE GANG'S MASTERMIND PLEADED GUILTY TO THE CRIME

TRIAL

The young man was extradited to the US and tried. He was accused of leading the IT attack on Citibank in New York City.

Although the hacker was found to have stolen more than $10 million and pleaded guilty, Levin was only sentenced to three years in jail and required to repay $240,015. Insurance companies had covered most of the stolen money.

The remaining members of the cybercrime gang were also caught and found guilty, but they are now all free.

THE HACKER THREAT

Hackers became a major threat for banks and companies, and they invested millions of dollars to set up new security systems to protect themselves from future cyberattacks.

It is, however, not always possible to outwit a hacker's skills and to thwart an attack, and one of the strategies used by some financial companies is therefore to hire the very hacker who had just attacked them.

TOWN AND COUNTRY

FEBRUARY 16, 2003
www.gva.be

DAILY NEWSPAPER NO. 152 - PRICE: Belgium € 2.50
Luxembourg € 2.30 - Netherlands € 3.20

GAZET VAN ANTWERPEN

DARING ATTACK ON THE WORLD DIAMOND CENTRE

LA SCUOLA DI TORINO
(THE SCHOOL OF TURIN) MANAGES TO OUTWIT THE WORLD'S MOST SOPHISTICATED SECURITY SYSTEM AND STEALS A STASH OF PRECIOUS STONES WORTH $100 MILLION

WHEN:	WHERE:	WHO:	LOOT:	OUTCOME:
THE WEEKEND OF FEBRUARY 15–16, 2003	WORLD DIAMOND CENTRE, ANTWERP, BELGIUM	LEONARDO NOTARBARTOLO AND HIS GANG, KNOWN AS LA SCUOLA DI TORINO	$100 MILLION WORTH OF GOLD, DIAMONDS, AND JEWELS	NOTARBARTOLO WAS SENTENCED TO 10 YEARS IN PRISON, AND THE REST OF THE GANG MEMBERS GOT FIVE YEARS

PLANNING THE ROBBERY

A TRUSTED DEALER IN ANTWERP'S DIAMOND DISTRICT

The Antwerp Diamond District, also known as the Diamond Quarter or the Square Mile, is the world's ultimate diamond-selling hot spot. Here the best specialists in the world cut and polish some 80 percent of the entire planet's gems.

In 2000, Leonardo Notarbartolo rented an office in the center of the famous district, passing himself off as an honest diamond dealer.

He would drink coffee and rub shoulders here with the biggest players of the diamond world, only to rob them later on, once he had gained their trust and friendship.

A BOLD PROPOSAL MADE BY A MYSTERIOUS SELLER

After he had stolen the precious stones, Notarbartolo sold them to "trusted" jewelers until, one day, an enigmatic dealer, who knew about the Italian's secret skills, made him a bold proposal:

"I WANT TO HIRE YOU FOR THE GREATEST DIAMOND ROBBERY IN HISTORY," HE TOLD HIM

His audacious proposal involved robbing the seemingly impenetrable vault of the Antwerp World Diamond Centre, with a stash of diamonds worth a colossal $100 million.

ALTHOUGH THE DISTRICT IS MONITORED 24/7 BY POLICE AND 63 SECURITY CAMERAS, IT IS A DREAM FOR THIEVES WITH MORE REFINED TASTES. NOTARBARTOLO MADE SURE HE WAS THERE FOR THE MEETING WITH THE SELLER

LEONARDO NOTARBARTOLO

A SNAKE CHARMER

The Italian crook ended up claiming he was born to steal. At the age of six, he robbed the local milkman while the latter was fast asleep, and that moment marked the start of an unstoppable career in crime.

Leonardo was a snake charmer, a sharp, handsome, sweet-talker who was able to gain anyone's trust . . . only to later steal his most valuable possessions.

NOTARBARTOLO SITTING IN A CAFÉ ON THE DIAMOND DISTRICT'S MAIN STREET, TALKING WITH ONE OF HIS CONTACTS ABOUT THE ROBBERY OF THE CENTURY.

PART ONE OF THE AGREEMENT

For €100,000 (approximately $160,000), he had to answer a simple question: Would it be possible to rob the vault of the World Diamond Centre, the most secure place in one of the most secure areas in the world? For such a sum, it was worth considering!

AN IMPOSSIBLE CHALLENGE

Before finally accepting the challenge, Notarbartolo studied all aspects of the heist. He could easily enter the center's vault, passing himself off as a client. He was known around the district for his honest business practices. Once inside, he used a small

camera hidden in his pen to photograph all the details of the vault. This would enable him to prove to the mysterious dealer that such a robbery was indeed going to be impossible.

THE WORLD DIAMOND CENTRE WAS AN IMPENETRABLE FORTRESS

The vault was located two levels belowground. It was protected by a 3-ton door, as well as motion, heat, and light sensors, and a lock with 100 million combinations and security cameras. It was the most secure, watertight vault on the planet.

A REPLICA VAULT MADE THE ROBBERY POSSIBLE

Six months later, however, the mysterious and tireless dealer had some surprising news for Notarbartolo. He had managed to build an exact replica of the World Diamond Centre's vault in an abandoned warehouse.

He informed Notarbartolo that he would just have to take charge of assembling a gang of the very best professionals he knew to commit the robbery. Once formed, the group would devote themselves to practicing on the replica vault until they had worked out how to get in without triggering any alarms.

THE DOOR HAD BEEN DESIGNED AND CONSTRUCTED TO WITHSTAND 12 HOURS OF CONTINUOUS DRILLING.

LA SCUOLA DI TORINO

NOTARBARTOLO ACCEPTED THE CHALLENGE AND RECRUITED

HIS CHOSEN MEMBERS MADE UP A GANG OF ITALIAN CROOKS KNOWN AS "LA SCUOLA DI TURINO"

The "Turin School" was a criminal gang of experts in alarm systems, door locks, and tunnels, capable of defying any challenger. Each was a master of his "art."

NOTARBARTOLO, Leonardo

FINOTTO, Ferdinando

D'ONORIO, Elio

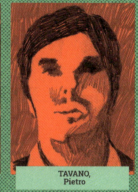
TAVANO, Pietro

UNKNOWN

LEONARDO NOTARBARTOLO

A stylish gentleman and master swindler. For more than two years, this crook from Turin played the role of a well-mannered Italian diamond trader in Antwerp's Diamond District. He masterminded the operation.

FERDINANDO FINOTTO
THE MONSTER

Ferdinando was tall and muscular. A skilled locksmith, electrician, mechanic, and driver, he was also a seasoned criminal whose failed attempt at bank robbery in 1997 served as training for his attack on the World Diamond Centre.

ELIO D'ONORIO
THE GENIUS

A specialist capable of disabling any kind of alarm, Elio found the most ingenious solutions to thwart the intimidating security measures at the World Diamond Centre.

PIETRO TAVANO
SPEEDY

Bad luck helped Pietro gain a reputation for ruining every robbery, but he was a loyal childhood friend of Notarbartolo's and a tireless accomplice in his misdeeds.

THE KING OF THE KEYS

Quite advanced in age, the unknown man was the best key-cutter in the world. He is the only gang member who was not caught and for whom no photograph exists.

METICULOUSLY STUDYING THE WORLD DIAMOND CENTRE

For months, Notarbartolo took charge of collecting detailed information about the vault. He made the most of his false identity as an honorable and trusted dealer to move freely in and out of the World Diamond Centre without ever raising any suspicions.

TRIAL RUNS OF THE HEIST IN THE DARK WITH THE VAULT REPLICA

The entire gang looked for weaknesses in the vault and prepared for the robbery in the replicated room. The specialists performed trial runs in the dark, combining their skills to perfect a plan capable of navigating the center's sophisticated security systems.

THE VAULT'S ENTRY CODE

In September 2002, one of the guards approached the door of the vault and started turning the dial on the combination lock. A miniature video camera had been installed by the gang and recorded his every move. With each turn, the dial stopped at a number. That's how the gang obtained the code.

ALL SET TO GET THE JOB DONE IN THE REAL VAULT

THE HEIST, STEP BY STEP

1. HEAT AND MOTION SENSORS

On February 14, Notarbartolo entered the World Diamond Centre's vault, as usual, without raising any suspicions.

Protected by his fake identity, he sprayed the heat and motion sensors with hair spray without anyone noticing.

A simple but very effective measure, it would prevent the alarm from going off right away, even if someone was to enter the vault.

ON HIS EARLIER VISITS TO THE VAULT NOTARBARTOLO HAD DONE THE GROUNDWORK FOR THE ROBBERY

2. THE DIAMOND DISTRICT, EMPTY

Two days later, helped by the fact that people in the district were preoccupied with a tennis final, the gang stormed the vault.

The robbers waited for nightfall. The moment the guards shut the steel doors at the entrance, the robbery began.

AT THAT HOUR, SECURITY WAS CONTROLLED ENTIRELY BY TECHNOLOGY, AND THAT WAS THE WEAKNESS EXPLOITED BY THE GANG

With the Diamond District empty, Notarbartolo drove his rented Peugeot 307 to a building located next to the World Diamond Centre. Out of the car jumped the Monster, the Genius, the King of Keys, and Speedy, Notarbartolo's childhood friend.

The King of Keys broke the lock and opened the door. The Genius went up to the rooftop and, from there, across to the World Diamond Centre, where he disabled a heat sensor, using a polyester shield, and entered. The other robbers followed him, covering the security cameras with black plastic.

They arrived at the vault, and the Genius began disabling the door's security mechanisms one by one. When the time came to open it with the security key, the King of Keys didn't have to do anything—the security guard had left the master key hanging on the wall. It seemed, for the moment, that luck was definitely on their side.

ALL THE TRIAL RUNS PREVIOUSLY PERFORMED AT THE DIAMOND CENTRE'S REPLICA VAULT WERE NOW BEARING THE HOPED-FOR RESULTS

3. A ROBBERY IN THE DARK

The gang managed to overcome all the security obstacles and enter the room. They worked in the dark and by memory, just as they had practiced. In the half-light of the vault, they opened more than 100 of the 189 safe-deposit boxes held there and loaded their bags with diamonds and jewels. At 5:30 a.m., before the district started coming to life, they left the World Diamond Centre with the booty.

NOT A SINGLE ALARM WENT OFF. THE ROBBERY HAD BEEN A SUCCESS!

Notarbartolo was waiting for the others at the end of the street in his rented Peugeot, listening to the police radio. The gang members jumped into his car, and they drove slowly away to their hideout.

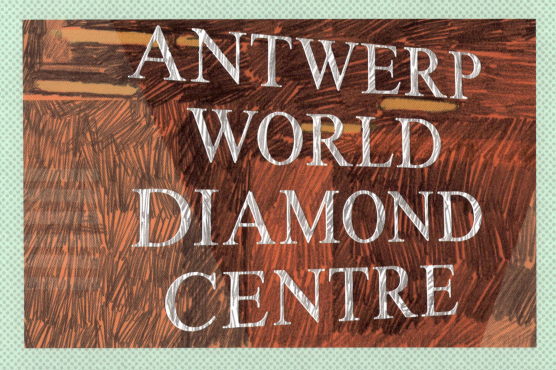

ANTWERP WORLD DIAMOND CENTRE

ON THE MORNING OF MONDAY, FEBRUARY 17, 2003, THE ANTWERP POLICE, WHO WERE IN CHARGE OF MONITORING THE DIAMOND DISTRICT AND ITS BUSINESSES, RECEIVED AN URGENT CALL: THERE HAD BEEN A ROBBERY AT THE WORLD DIAMOND CENTRE.

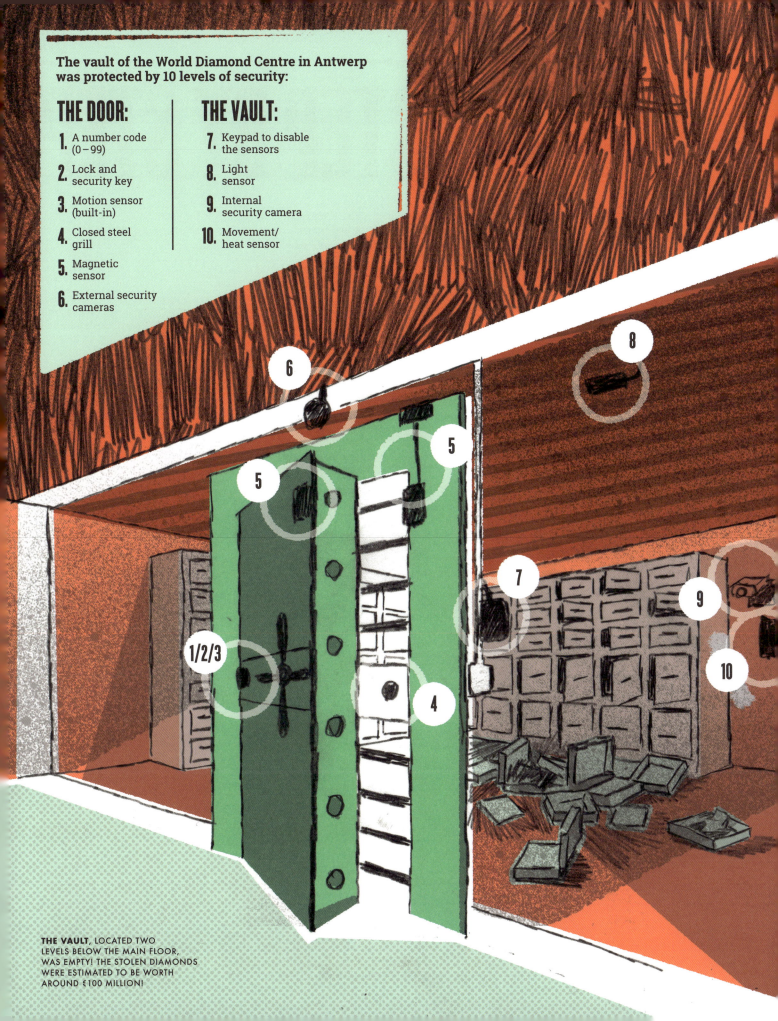

The vault of the World Diamond Centre in Antwerp was protected by 10 levels of security:

THE DOOR:

1. A number code (0–99)
2. Lock and security key
3. Motion sensor (built-in)
4. Closed steel grill
5. Magnetic sensor
6. External security cameras

THE VAULT:

7. Keypad to disable the sensors
8. Light sensor
9. Internal security camera
10. Movement/ heat sensor

THE VAULT, LOCATED TWO LEVELS BELOW THE MAIN FLOOR, WAS EMPTY! THE STOLEN DIAMONDS WERE ESTIMATED TO BE WORTH AROUND €100 MILLION!

4. THE MYSTERIOUS TRADER HAD TRICKED THEM

Once in the safety of their hideout, the thieves opened the bags they had filled in the dark. To their surprise, most of the bags were totally empty!

Something had gone wrong. Instead of the $100 million they had been promised by the enigmatic trader, they had only $20 million.

That's when the gang realized that the mysterious diamond trader had tricked them.

NOTARBARTOLO HAD BEEN SCAMMED. HE HAD GOTTEN A TASTE OF HIS OWN MEDICINE

The trader had secretly taken the diamonds out before the robbery. Since there were no clues to the whereabouts of the diamonds, the insurance company paid out compensation to the center's victims. The robbery was a cover for a million-euro compensation claim for supposedly stolen diamonds, and Notarbartolo had been conned.

IT WAS NOT A DIAMOND ROBBERY. IT WAS ACTUALLY THE BIGGEST INSURANCE SCAM IN HISTORY

5. THE ESCAPE AND SPEEDY'S MISFORTUNE

Notarbartolo and his loyal friend Speedy hastily fled the city with their share of the booty. They were headed toward Italy.

Along the way, they decided to get rid of the wrapping around the diamonds. They stopped the car, ready to burn the evidence. But suddenly, they heard a sound, Speedy panicked, and they left without finishing the job. After committing a perfect robbery, Speedy's bad luck once again thwarted them—a gust of wind scattered the wrapping, covered with their fingerprints, all over the place.

The man who had made the noise that startled Speedy and Notarbartolo while they were trying to destroy the evidence had been out hunting weasels.

When he saw the scattered wrapping the next morning, he contacted the police, who were immediately struck by the fact that some of the envelopes bore the seal of the Antwerp World Diamond Centre.

SPEEDY'S BLUNDER LED THE POLICE STRAIGHT TO NOTARBARTOLO

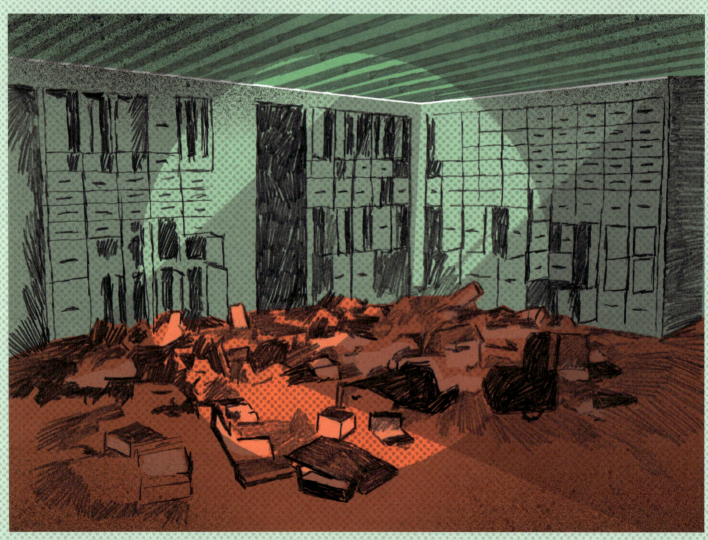

THE STATE OF THE VAULT, LOCATED IN THE BASEMENT OF THE WORLD DIAMOND CENTRE, AFTER THE ROBBERY.

POLICE INVESTIGATION & OUTCOME

The evidence scattered all over the highway was sufficient for the police to catch the gang. Only the wily old King of Keys managed to escape the law.

NOTARBARTOLO WAS ARRESTED AFTER THE POLICE MANAGED TO LINK HIM TO THE ROBBERY BASED ON DNA EVIDENCE THAT WAS FOUND ON A HALF-EATEN SANDWICH NEAR THE CRIME SCENE, AS WELL AS VIDEOTAPES FROM THE DIAMOND CENTRE

THE OUTCOME

Leonardo Notarbartolo was sentenced to 10 years in prison by the Belgian court. The rest of the gang members spent five years each behind bars.

THE LOOT

The diamonds were never recovered. To this day, they might still be hidden somewhere in the rugged terrain of the Alps.

For his part in the robbery, the enigmatic diamond trader vanished without a single trace, never to be seen again.

THE PLACE NEAR HIGHWAY E19, NORTH OF BRUSSELS, WHERE SPEEDY THREW OUT THE TRASH BAG CONTAINING THE DIAMONDS' WRAPPING.

ISSN 1517-6819

O POVO

FORTALEZA-CE, Sunday, August 7, 2005 YEAR LXXVIII No. 25.664 RS 2.00

86 -PAGE EDITION

INCREDIBLE!
164 MILL. REALS STOLEN

FROM FORTALEZA'S BANCO CENTRAL THROUGH A 260-FOOT-LONG TUNNEL

A COLOSSAL FEAT OF ENGINEERING MADE THIS ROBBERY ONE OF THE MOST SPECTACULAR IN THE HISTORY OF BRAZIL

THE CITY OF FORTALEZA IS ON THE NORTHEAST COAST OF BRAZIL.

THE BANCO CENTRAL BUILDING IN FORTALEZA.

WHEN:	WHERE:	WHO:	LOOT:	OUTCOME:
AUGUST 6 AND 7, 2005	BANCO CENTRAL OF FORTALEZA, BRAZIL	A GANG OF 35 MEN	164 MILLION REALS ($29 MILLION)	ONLY SOME OF THE GANG WERE CAUGHT. THE MOST SEVERE SENTENCE—49 YEARS' IMPRISONMENT—WAS GIVEN TO THE LEADER, KNOWN AS "THE GERMAN"

PLANNING THE ROBBERY

THE IDEA

Legend has it that the idea to rob Fortaleza's Banco Central was first conceived by the security guards of a transport company, who worked for the institution.

It was these guards who, while visiting the home city of "the German" (the alias used by Antônio Jussivan Alves dos Santos), proposed the plan to him.

THE AIM WAS TO EMPTY THE SAFES OF THE BANCO CENTRAL'S UNDERGROUND VAULT VIA A LONG TUNNEL

CONFIDENTIAL INFORMATION

The German accepted the challenge and over the following months, he began to collect detailed information on the exact location of the bank's various coffers, security cameras, intruder alarms, motion sensors, and crates of money.

IT WAS SUCH A CRAZY FEAT. IT WAS LIKE SOMETHING OUT OF A MOVIE, BUT IT WAS NOT IMPOSSIBLE, AND IT ALSO RELIED ON ACCOMPLICES WITHIN THE BANK

A PROFESSIONAL TEAM

The German recruited a gang of specialists in various fields for the great "coup."

Among them, he employed engineers, excavators, forgers, and big-time investors who put up the money to build the super-expensive tunnel that would lead them to the bank's coffers.

SMOKE SCREEN

It was also essential to create a smoke screen to act as a cover for the great feat of engineering that would lead them to the Banco Central's underground vault.

The robbers rented a small house near the bank and hung up a sign outside, claiming to be a gardening company. They also wore the clothes typical of professional gardeners, and their trucks bore the company's logo on the side.

This fake business enabled the crooks to remove the dirt they dug up without raising suspicion among the neighbors.

Everything was perfectly organized so that the gang could get straight to work excavating the tunnel.

THE HOUSE FROM WHICH THEY STARTED DIGGING THE TUNNEL WAS TURNED INTO A GARDENING COMPANY SPECIALIZING IN LAWN CARE

FROM THE HOUSE THEY HAD RENTED NEAR THE BANK, THE GANG SPENT THREE MONTHS DIGGING A 260-FOOT-LONG TUNNEL TO THE VAULT. ON THE WEEKEND OF AUGUST 6 AND 7, 2005, THEY MADE THEIR WAY INTO THE VAULT AND STOLE THE MODERN-DAY EQUIVALENT OF AROUND $29 MILLION.

THE HEIST, STEP BY STEP

1. A TUNNEL TO THE BANK

A gang of 10 began tirelessly working on the underground passage. Every day, the fake gardeners would remove large quantities of dirt, which they transported away in trucks.

Just as they had intended, this earth-moving work did not attract any attention from the neighbors, who figured it was a perfectly normal activity for a gardening company.

The gang managed to dig the tunnel in three months. In the process, they had to pass beneath one of the city's main streets (the wide Avenida Dom Manuel) to get to the bank.

2. A FEAT OF ENGINEERING

30
TONS OF DIRT REMOVED

87
YARDS OF TUNNEL

WOODEN BRACING TO PREVENT THE TUNNEL'S COLLAPSING

VENTILATION AND AIR-CONDITIONING

TUNNEL LIGHTING SYSTEM

3. ARMORED VAULT

When the gang reached the floor of the bank, they stopped and waited for the weekend before entering the vault.

The vault was protected by 3.6 feet of steel-reinforced concrete. In order to get through the base plate into the interior of the chamber, the men needed diamond drills, bolt cutters, and rubber-clad electric saws to muffle the noise.

THE GANG MANAGED TO GET THROUGH WITHOUT AN ALARM GOING OFF. THEY HAD MADE IT IN!

IT WAS AN IMPRESSIVE FEAT THAT COST A VERITABLE FORTUNE

4. PAUSING THE SECURITY CAMERAS

The vault was in a large 5,400-square-foot room, and every inch of it was monitored by security cameras. Yet thanks to the gangsters' accomplices within the bank, the cameras could be paused for the duration of the robbery.

5. THE LOOT

The burglars had a field day, opening the bank's five safes that contained millions in used 50-real bills. These banknotes had been set aside to analyze whether they could be put back in circulation or whether they should be burned, based on the condition they were in.

THE BANKNOTES WERE FROM AN UNKNOWN SERIES THAT THE POLICE COULD NOT TRACE

6. LOADING THE LOOT

The robbers spent seven hours loading three tons of bills onto carts on ropes that formed part of a pulley system, which they used to haul the cash through the tunnel to their house.

7. THE ESCAPE

From the house, they loaded the money onto trucks. They abandoned their tools in the tunnel, and after spraying the house with lime to get rid of any fingerprints, they fled in the quiet hours of the early morning.

Within hours of the bank's opening, the gang was dividing up their 164 million reals before they disbanded.

THE BURGLARS ALL TRAVELED TO DIFFERENT PARTS OF THE COUNTRY

THE INSIDE OF THE 260-FOOT-LONG TUNNEL ILLUMINATED AND BRACED.

THE ROUTE TO THE LOOT

ALL THE BILLS WERE USED 50-REAL BANKNOTES, AND WERE POSSIBLY DUE TO BE REMOVED FROM CIRCULATION. IT IS SUSPECTED THAT BANK EMPLOYEES—NOT JUST SECURITY STAFF—WERE ACCOMPLICES IN THE ROBBERY. THREE MILLION BILLS WERE STOLEN, WEIGHING THREE TONS.

THE VAULT

The thieves drilled through the 12-foot-thick walls to gain access to the room.

THE BANCO CENTRAL'S VAULT

BUILDING UNDER CONSTRUCTION

TUNNEL

Av. Dom Manuel

Av. Heráclito Graça

ROOM WHERE SEVERAL SACKS OF SAND WERE FOUND

ROOM WHERE THE TUNNEL STARTED

KITCHEN

ENTRANCE

The tunnel was accessed from inside the house.

HOUSE FROM WHERE THE THIEVES DUG THE TUNNEL

HOTEL

STORES (MOSTLY CLOSED)

Calle 25 de Marzo

GANG MEMBERS WHO HAVE BEEN IDENTIFIED:

ANTÔNIO JUSSIVAN ALVES
THE GERMAN, LEADER OF THE GANG

He admitted having been involved and having received 5 million reals but never acknowledged his role as the gang's leader. He was sentenced to 49 years and two months in jail, the most severe of all the penalties.

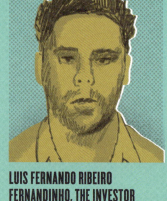

LUIS FERNANDO RIBEIRO
FERNANDINHO, THE INVESTOR

He financed the robbery. While the police never managed to catch him, he was kidnapped and executed by another gang despite the 2-million-real ransom paid by his family.

ANTÔNIO ARGEU NUNES VIEIRA
THE INVESTOR

The former mayor of the city of Boa Viagem (Ceará), he was imprisoned for having financed the robbery but was eventually set free due to a lack of evidence.

MOISÉS TEIXEIRA DA SILVA
THE EXCAVATOR

Considered one of the gang's main ringleaders, he was caught, thanks to an undercover agent at the bakery he used to frequent. He was sentenced to 17 years in prison but was released after only two.

MARCOS ROGÉRIO MACHADO DE MORAIS
THE ENGINEER

An engineer by profession, this gang member was imprisoned, but he managed to escape after serving just a few years of his sentence. To this day, the whereabouts of Marco Rogério are unknown.

JOSÉ CHARLES MACHADO DE MORAIS
THE LAUNDERER

The owner of a transport company and the brother of Marco Rogério (the Engineer), he was sentenced to 36 years in prison, accused of laundering the stolen money. He escaped in a notorious prison break, along with eight other criminals.

JORGE LUIZ DA SILVA
THE FORGER

He was the gang member in charge of producing the falsified documents needed to set up the fake gardening company that served as a cover for the robbery. He ended up in prison.

DEUCIMAR NEVES QUEIROZ
THE INFORMER

A former security guard at Fortaleza's Banco Central, he informed the gang of the exact location of the vault, security cameras, alarms, motion sensors, and stacks of money. He received 2 million reals of the booty, but he could not evade the police and eventually ended up in jail.

FUGITIVES AND THE MISSING LOOT

While there were many who ended up in prison following the Fortaleza Banco Central robbery, others remained free, particularly those from the higher echelons of society, whom nobody dared accuse.

What's more, only about 10 percent of the stolen money was ever recovered. Somewhere in the world, the "big fish" of this robbery are free and enjoying the money, while others are serving long jail terms.

THE MOVIE

The 2011 Brazilian thriller *Asalto al Banco Central (Federal Bank Heist)*, directed by Marcos Paulo, was based on this robbery.

POLICE INVESTIGATION

THE BIGGEST ROBBERY IN BRAZIL'S HISTORY

The bank opened its doors on Monday, August 8.

THE VAULT HAD BEEN DRILLED THROUGH AND A NEW TUNNEL LED OUT OF THE CHAMBER

Several fearless agents then volunteered to explore the underground passage. The police feared that the robbers might have laid traps throughout the tunnel, but the agents braved the dark, 260-foot-long shaft to find out where it led.

THE FAKE GARDENING COMPANY BECAME THE FOCUS OF THE INVESTIGATION

Painstakingly, the police began reconstructing all the facts of the crime, while the neighbors were shocked to realize that for months they had been witnessing up close an extraordinary feat of engineering that had facilitated the crime.

ANTONIO CELSO DOS SANTOS, MEMBER OF THE FEDERAL POLICE.

THE TUNNEL BECAME A LEGEND

The daring heist made headlines in all the papers. The gang had stolen 164 million reals from the Banco Central by digging a 260-foot-long tunnel to escape.

HAVING NOT ISSUED ANY THREATS OR FIRED ANY SHOTS OR SET OFF ANY ALARMS, THE ROBBERY WENT DOWN AS THE LARGEST AND MOST SOPHISTICATED IN BRAZIL'S HISTORY

THE FEDERAL POLICE

Antonio Celso Dos Santos, a well-regarded member of Brazil's Federal Police, along with his team of trusted officers, was put in charge of investigating the bank robbery.

A FEW MILLION-DOLLAR MISTAKES

Despite the great care taken by the gang, Antonio Dos Santos's team of police officers was able to find fingerprints of one of the thieves in the house. They belonged to José Marleudo, the German's brother-in-law.

A few days later, another gang member bought 10 cars with 50-real bills in cash. His name was José Charles Machado de Morais, and the police knew immediately that he must also have been involved in the robbery.

It was these two robbers, José Marleudo and José Charles Machado de Morais, who eventually led the police to the rest of the gang.

WANTED:

BRUCE REYNOLDS

A GANG OF 15 MEN, LED BY BRUCE REYNOLDS, ROBBED THE GLASGOW-TO-LONDON ROYAL MAIL TRAIN.

£2.6 MILLION

VINCENZO PERUGGIA

A HUMBLE CARPENTER MANAGED TO EXPLOIT THE FLAWS IN THE LOUVRE'S SECURITY SYSTEM.

THE THEFT OF THE *MONA LISA*

DIONISIO RODRÍGUEZ MARTÍN
EL DIONI

OVERNIGHT, EL DIONI WENT FROM BEING AN ANONYMOUS WORKER TO SPAIN'S MOST FAMOUS MILLIONAIRE FUGITIVE.

320 MILLION PESETAS

VLADIMIR LEVIN

A YOUNG MAN OUTWITS CITIBANK'S TECH SECURITY.

$10.7 MILLON

ALBERT SPAGGIARI

"NO WEAPONS, NO VIOLENCE, AND NO HATRED."

HE ROBBED THE BANK OF NICE OF THE EQUIVALENT OF MORE THAN $11 MILLION IN MONEY AND JEWELS

2 UNIDENTIFIED BURGLARS

CONSIDERED THE GREATEST ART ROBBERY IN US HISTORY, THE FBI HAS YET TO SOLVE THIS CASE.

13 WORKS OF ART WORTH $500 MILLION

DAN COOPER

DAN COOPER THREATENED TO BLOW UP A SEATTLE-BOUND BOEING 727.

HE SECURED A BOOTY OF $200,000

LEONARDO NOTARBARTOLO
LA SCUOLA DI TORINO

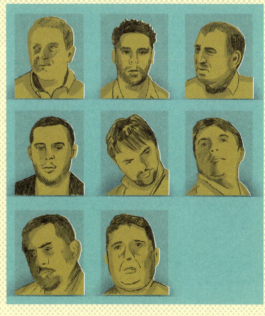

A GANG OF 35 MEN LED BY

ANTÔNIO JUSSIVAN ALVES
THE GERMAN

DESPITE THE DISTRICT'S BEING CLOSELY MONITORED BY THE POLICE AND 63 SECURITY CAMERAS 24 HOURS A DAY, LEONARDO NOTARBARTOLO DARED TO ROB THE WORLD DIAMOND CENTRE.

100 MILLION WORTH OF DIAMONDS AND JEWELS

THEY ROBBED FORTALEZA'S BANCO CENTRAL VIA A 260-FOOT-LONG TUNNEL.

164 MILLION REALS